Mort Künstler's

OLD WEST

INDIANS

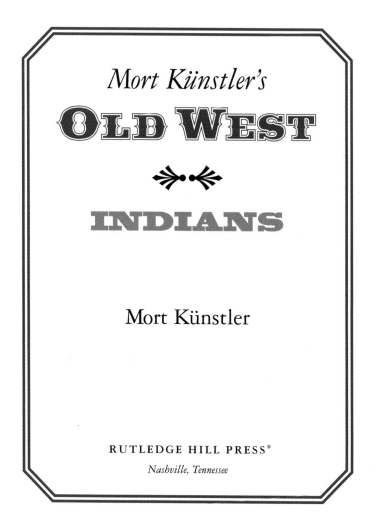

Mort Künstler's

OLD WEST

INDIANS

Mort Künstler

RUTLEDGE HILL PRESS®

Nashville, Tennessee

Published by Rutledge Hill Press®, 211 Seventh Avenue North, Nashville, Tennessee
37219. Distributed in Canada by H. B. Fenn & Company, Ltd., 34 Nixon Road,
Bolton, Ontario L7E 1W2. Distributed in Australia by Five Mile Press Pty., Ltd.,
22 Summit Road, Noble Park, Victoria 3174. Distributed in New Zealand by
Tandem Press, 2 Rugby Road, Birkenhead, Auckland 10. Distributed in the
United Kingdom by Verulam Publishing, Ltd., 152a Park Street Lane, Park Street,
St. Albans, Hertfordshire AL2 2AU.

Jacket and text design by Bruce Gore / Gore Studio, Inc.
Color separations by NEC Incorporated

Library of Congress Cataloging-in-Publication Data

Künstler, Mort.
   [Old West]
   Mort Künstler's Old West. Indians / Mort Künstler
      p.   cm.
   A collection of Mort Künstler's paintings depicting Indian life of the Old West.
   ISBN 1-55853-589-6 (hb)
   1. Künstler, Mort—Catalogs.   2. Indians of North America—Pictorial
works—Catalogs.   3. West (U.S.)—In art—Catalogs.
I. Title.
ND237.K85A4   1998a
759.13—dc21   98-15248
                                            CIP

Printed in the United States of America
1 2 3 4 5 6 7 8 9 — 02 01 00 99 98

Especially for
DAVID *and* PAT

※◆※

Contents

Introduction

✦

BEFORE THE discovery of North America by Europeans, a large population of native Americans inhabited this vast continent. They were separated into a multitude of tribes and nations that were as diverse in language and customs as the countries of Europe. As is well known, Christopher Columbus called them "Indians" because he mistakenly thought he had discovered a western route to India. The name, as wrong as it is, has stuck. I hope my native American friends will understand why, for the sake of easy identification, I use the word "Indian" in this book.

My first introduction to native Americans was the same as everyone else in my generation—through the movies. As a kid growing up in Brooklyn in the 1930s and 1940s, I spent Saturday afternoons at the movies watching the Marx Brothers or westerns. Playing cowboys and Indians was a popular street game, and in those days, the Indians were almost always the "bad guys." Not until years later did the public in general start to view the clash between whites and Indians as a great cultural conflict in which there were "good guys" and "bad guys" on both sides. The truth is that both cultures acted in ways that were dictated by their respective societies. Throughout history there have always been cultural conflicts, and the results have never been pleasant for the vanquished. I have tried to show this conflict of cultures realistically in the paintings in this book.

I have also tried to show how inappropriate some of the popular misconceptions about native Americans are. We tend to think of them as one giant monolithic group called "Indians," when in reality native American cultural groups were as diverse as the European civilization that invaded North America. I became aware of their diversity when Readers Digest Books commissioned me to do a painting of Haida Indians, a Northwest coastal tribe. Their richly carved totem poles and lodges, highly developed art, complex ceremonies, and sophisticated religion were as developed and civilized as any at the fabled court of King Arthur.

The Apache in the Southwest developed a society that was adapted to their natural habitat. The Plains Indians, those we think of as wearing the elaborate feathered headdress, did the same. They became a buffalo culture, obtaining their food, clothing, and shelter from the massive bison herds that roamed the Great Plains. In the portrait gallery at the back of this book, I emphasize the enormous differences that existed in native American tribal societies long before whites explored and settled North America.

In this book, *Mort Künstler's Old West: Indians,* and its companion book, *Mort Künstler's Old West: Cowboys*, I have selected paintings from the hundreds I have done over a period of more than forty-five years to bring some of the danger, excitement, and adventure of the West to others.

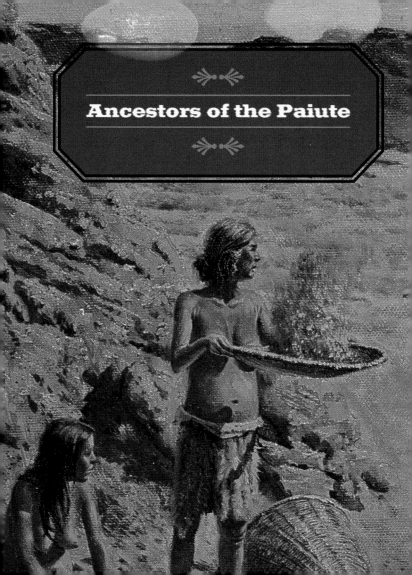

Ancestors of the Paiute

The concept for this painting came about when a publisher commissioned a painting of Haida Indians, a Northwest coastal tribe. The idea was to divide the book into ten chapters representing different geographic areas and showing how native Americans adapted to their diverse environments. This painting was

to be the opener for the Southwest chapter. Although the book project did not work out, I finished all ten of the paintings. I chose five of them as the central theme of my first exhibition at Hammer Galleries in New York City in 1977.

The setting is the Four Corners region, where the state lines of Utah, Colorado, Arizona, and New Mexico meet. This scene shows cave-dwelling Indians, the ancestors of the Paiute, before the arrival of the white man.

The early Paiutes were hunter-gatherers and cave-dwellers from about 350 B.C. They slept in holes scratched in the ground and sustained themselves on a diet of insects, field mice, and weed seeds. They did not experience contact with whites until the 1820s.

Although the Paiutes were primarily seed gatherers, a successful hunt was always cause for great excitement. We see that excitement as the returning hunters bring in their bountiful prize. The women on the ground stretch antelope skins from a previous hunt.

Paiutes chose caves that faced west to take advantage of the warmth of the afternoon sun. In this scene I show the typical tasks the Paiutes would be doing. In the left foreground, a man makes decoys out of tule for duck hunting. The man directly behind him mends a net for catching rabbits. One man starts a fire with the help of the boy blowing on the sparks. The standing woman is catching the natural breeze to winnow seed from chaff, and the seated woman is working with a mortar and pestle to make meal. The Paiute were such skilled basket weavers that the tightly woven water basket carried by the young girl in the right foreground does not leak.

Preliminary charcoal sketch

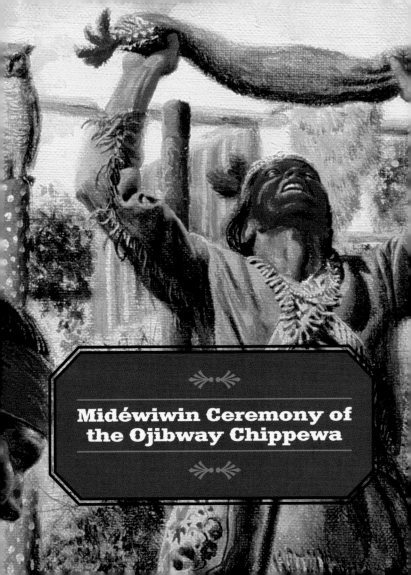

Midéwiwin Ceremony of the Ojibway Chippewa

This painting depicts the ceremonial lodge of the Ojibway Chippewa, a tribe from the Great Lakes region. It shows the initiation of a new member into the Midéwiwin, an exclusive society of shamans or medicine men.

White Americans first came to know the Ojibway Chippewa through Longfellow's epic poem "The Song of Hiawatha." In the seventeenth century the Ojibway were perhaps the largest native American group, numbering around thirty-five thousand. They thrived in northern Michigan, Wisconsin, and Minnesota as late as the early nineteenth century. When white settlement encroached on their hunting ground, many Ojibway moved to North Dakota, Montana, and Ontario, rarely involving themselves in violence against the paleskinned newcomers. They prospered because of their political skill.

In this scene, a novice kneels and is held in place by two Midéwiwin as his mentor shoots a cowrie shell or "migi" from an otter-skin bag. Chants and music accompany the ceremony. Later, a healer will extract the evil spirit from the initiate. The ceremony lasted several days and involved the purification, instruction, and initiation of the novice.

There were four degrees of the Midéwiwin. Each one was more powerful than the previous, and in our society would be equivalent to the levels of elementary school, middle school, high school, and college. The four poles in the rear of the ceremonial lodge represent the four grades of the society. Members showed their rank by painting designs and colors on their faces.

I did most of the research for this painting at the Museum of Natural History in New York City. I believe this was the first time a painting had been done of this elaborate and colorful ritual.

Preliminary pencil drawing

Tomahawk Throwing Contest

In the early 1800s white trappers extended their interests into the country's unexplored interior. Occasionally, British companies sponsored large meetings with the trappers to buy their pelts. French-Canadian trappers called the event a "rendezvous." These British-sponsored meetings were infrequent, but in 1825 an American fur trader, William H. Ashley, revised the rendezvous. His first meeting was a modest success. The following year he held another rendezvous and also sold potent potables, making an enormous profit. The trappers spent almost all the cash they had earned from furs to buy whiskey and trinkets for their Indian companions. The mountain men spent several days at Ashley's camp gambling and challenging each other to games of frontier skill.

There have been many paintings of mountain men during a rendezvous. A natural diversion would have been a tomahawk-throwing contest with a lot of betting on the outcome. I decided to paint such a contest after spending some time with a reenactment group of mountain men near Tucson. I had never seen a painting of a tomahawk-throwing contest.

This painting is one of the most difficult I have ever done, and I believe it is one of my most successful works. Note how many different types of men attended the rendezvous and that, for a brief moment in time, many cultures coexisted and blended.

Preliminary charcoal sketch

War Cry

Pounding hooves and blood-curdling screams were the nightmare of almost all whites in the West during the nineteenth century. To bring an event like this attack to canvas, I first had to choose which tribe to depict. The Sioux, or Lakota, were famous for their warlike natures. They were feared by neighboring tribes as much as by the whites. The Sioux

terrorized cowboys in raids on the Bozeman Trail, killed soldiers in entrapments like the 1866 Fetterman Massacre, and, led by the chief called Red Cloud, killed and harassed whites in the Powder River War of 1866–68. The Teton Sioux followed Crazy Horse and Sitting Bull to battles at Rosebud Creek and the Little Bighorn River in the 1870s.

The Sioux depicted here are wearing feathered warbonnets, buffalo or medicine hats, and beaded breastplates. They carry stone-tipped lances, war clubs, and the long, curved coup stick—all relics of a time when the Sioux turned their fury on their traditional enemies, the Pawnee and the Crow. The symbolic headgear indicates that these warriors possess powerful medicine or magic, the breastplate turns away the arrows of the enemy, and the coup stick is for striking the inept opponent and showing him that the Sioux disdain him and his fighting skills. They also carry mid-1870s vintage Winchester repeating carbines, weapons purchased from traders or taken from settlers or cattlemen slain in raids.

I felt that a long, narrow composition was perfect for focusing in on a large number of Indians with their horses. This approach let me show many exciting actions of both horses and men and also show various types of weapons, war paint, decorations, and accouterments. Choosing a dry riverbed for the action allows the eye to focus on the figures and horses in an action-packed, complete composition within a very simple environment.

Painted Horse

This composition is one of the few times when a large, complicated painting has served as the preliminary to one of my smaller paintings. After finishing *War Cry*, I was so interested in the subject matter that I created a smaller, less complicated painting focused on one Indian. I was intrigued by the warrior holding his Winchester high over his head. I like this painting as much as I like *War Cry*. I call it *Painted Horse* after the war-painted Pinto the warrior rides; Painted Horse could also be the name of the brave.

The painted handprints on the chests of the warriors' horses record how many men the riders have killed in hand-to-hand combat. Before the Sioux rode horses, these handprints were put on the chests of the warriors themselves.

Eagle feathers worn in the warriors' hair mean they have counted coup—vanquished their enemies, literally or symbolically—and these acts have been witnessed by other braves. The feathers do not represent empty boasts; they are proof that these warriors have been tested in battle. Decorations demonstrated the bravery, ferocity, and deadliness of the braves, and they made the hearts of soldiers sink.

A few teenage Sioux boys took part in the battle of the Little Bighorn, and in their old age they told how they prepared for the fight. One, called Wooden Leg, recalled how he put on his best shirt, moccasins, and breeches and then applied his war colors, painting a blue and black circle around his entire face and filling in the center with red and yellow. The idea was to present a fierce face to the enemy, a face as fierce as that of the lead rider in this painting—a man whose face is painted blood red from his hairline to his chin.

Treaty Talk

This painting evolved in 1978 from an idea given to me by the late John Davidson of Vancouver. He visited me at my studio in Oyster Bay, New York, and bought several of my paintings, including one, still unfinished, that stood on the easel. He not only suggested the idea for this composition but also the title. John later bought this painting when I finished it in 1979. Today it is part of a collection

of my works bequeathed by Mr. Davidson to the Glenbow Museum in Calgary.

This painting does not depict a specific event but represents hundreds of similar incidents that occurred throughout the West during the Indian wars. These U.S. officers and cavalry troopers wear the uniform of the late 1870s, but this small treaty discussion could have taken place at any time between 1865 and 1891.

Treaty discussions often established new boundaries for hunting or new sites for reservations. Treaty negotiations, however, were not always safe situations for either tribal or military representatives. The Apache chief Cochise embarked on his wars with the United States after an army lieutenant with whom he was engaged in a treaty discussion imprisoned him until Cochise agreed to his terms and confessed to a crime he did not commit. Maj. Gen. Edward R. S. Canby was killed during negotiations with hostile Modoc tribesmen in 1873.

I used late-afternoon sunlight to create a pattern of light and dark, and I purposely placed the Indians in complete shadow. This use of light enabled me to make even the white headdress of the main Indian darker than the mountains in the background, creating an interesting and dramatic effect. The mountains on the left and right create a "V" with the chief officer and the tribal representative at its base, leading the viewer's eye to the center of interest.

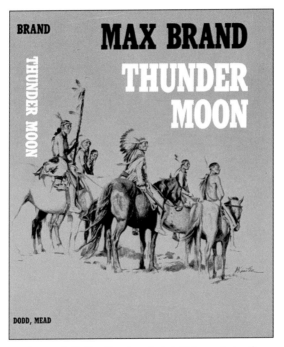

For the cover of this Max Brand novel, the publisher used a pencil study I had made for Treaty Talk.

Apache Feet Leave
No Trail

I was driving

through central Arizona when I came across this rocky outcropping. I stopped the car, wandered around looking at the scenery, took some photographs, and eventually came back to this site. It made me realize how the

Apache could so easily disappear when necessary. Familiar with the land, they could hide practically under the noses of their pursuers. I took out my sketch pad and immediately envisioned a company of cavalry on the top of the rocks looking for an Apache brave hiding directly below it.

This Apache is practicing the concealment skills his people used during their 250-year war with the white man. Famous for their stealth, ferocity, horsemanship, and cruelty, the Apache probably took their name from the Navaho word *apachu*, meaning "the enemy."

It was believed and regularly demonstrated that an Apache warrior—often clothed in only a breechcloth, calf-high soft leather boots, and headband—could disappear in the middle of a barren desert landscape. Frightened and superstitious whites believed Apache could transform into rocks, cactus, or the sand beneath their feet. Disguised in this way, if he had a knife, the Apache would kill you. If he did not have a knife, he would take your horse and water.

This painting was done as a sequel to *When You Can't Hide Your Tracks* to show how different weather conditions influenced the outcome of many clashes. It was a very difficult story to tell because the Indian had to be well hidden from his pursuers, which also means it should be difficult for the viewer to see him. I thought a touch of sunlight hitting his headband would create a brilliant spot of red, drawing the eye to the hidden warrior. I also felt that it would be an interesting painting even if the viewer did not see the Apache. I finally decided against using the bright red, knowing full well that the warrior would not have allowed himself to be seen.

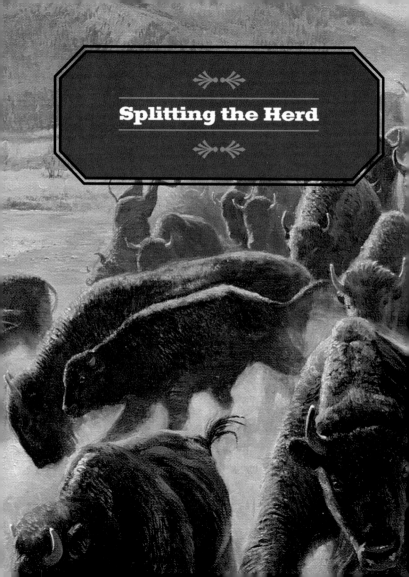

Splitting the Herd

I visited Yellowstone in 1987 with my good friend Jim Court, a former park ranger. While traveling through the beautiful La Mar Valley, we came across a small herd of bison. We had already seen many of these majestic animals, but the setting was so magnificent that in spite of rules about visitors' staying in their cars, I jumped out and began visualizing a painting. In my mind's eye, the road and the cars became an enormous buffalo herd during an Indian attack. The sunlight bouncing off the river was just right; the colors of the grass, sky, and animals were perfect. I began sketching and took photographs in preparation for a painting I knew I would do soon.

In the early seventeenth century, as many as 40 million bison grazed the plains from Mexico to Canada. About that time, the Plains Indians started using horses for hunting. Mounted and armed with only lances or arrows, the tribes of the Great Plains perfected buffalo hunting.

This painting shows a small party of Crow engaged in a typical but dramatic hunting maneuver. This was one of the most effective methods mounted Plains Indians used to hunt. Translated from several Indian languages as "the surround," the tactic called for two lines of mounted men to charge a herd of buffalo from opposite directions, gallop around it in an ever-restricting circle, and kill the herd's leader. As the remaining bulls and cows panicked, the riders bisected the herd, firing arrows or lancing animals as they went.

Armed with heavy-caliber rifles, the whites one day would hunt these beasts into near extinction. By the 1890s the Canadian government established an Alberta preserve to nurture its last herd of wild bison. The United States soon followed, setting up one bison preserve in western Montana and another in Yellowstone National Park.

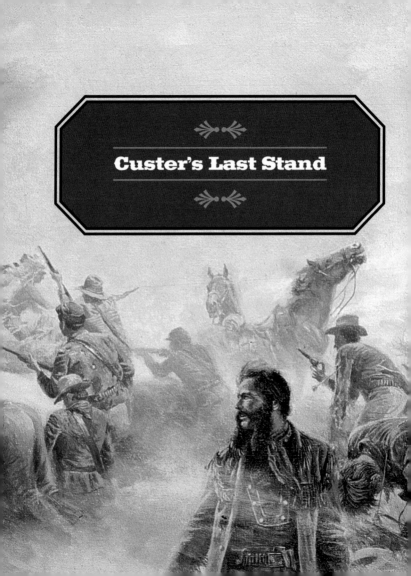

Custer's Last Stand

On the afternoon of June 25, 1876, 261 men of the U.S. Seventh Cavalry led by Gen. George Armstrong Custer were massacred near the banks of the Little Bighorn River in Montana. The numerically superior force of Sioux and Cheyenne warriors was organized by the Sioux leader Sitting Bull and led by the war chief Crazy Horse.

After a short pursuit by the warriors, Custer's command made a stand on the small rise shown here. The actions and general positions of the last living cavalrymen are corroborated by archaeological evidence and Sioux and Cheyenne oral histories and drawings. No one of Custer's force survived the encounter.

I visited the Custer Battlefield National Monument for the first time in 1984 to research the terrain where the famous fight took place. I met the superintendent of the site, Jim Court, and Neil Mangum, the battlefield's chief historian at the time, and it seemed that I asked them a million questions. Jim and I spent so much time together that we have been very good friends since that day.

Back in my studio I did a small study that was used on a postal commemorative cover. After several years of digesting the material I had gathered and additional trips to the battlefield, I embarked on a major canvas that was one of the most difficult paintings I have ever done.

To begin with, Custer's Last Stand has been painted by artists as renowned as W. R. Leigh, A. R. Waud, and E. S. Paxon. Because I had more facts than any artist before me, I believed I could do the most accurate painting ever done of Custer's last battle.

I checked my facts constantly, and I painted for what seemed like endless weeks. When I finally finished, I sent a photograph to Neil and Jim. Neil was highly critical of most paintings, and he always found inaccuracies. When I received the letter on the following page, I was more than rewarded for my effort.

The painting was made into a limited-edition print to benefit the Custer Battlefield Preservation Committee. It sold out quickly and helped raise thousands of dollars to buy land adjacent to the battlefield. This is indeed one of the most satisfying paintings I have ever done.

United States Department of the Interior

NATIONAL PARK SERVICE
Custer Battlefield National Monument
Post Office Box 39
Crow Agency, Montana 59022

IN REPLY REFER TO:
A52 (CUST)

September 10, 1986

Mr. Mort Kunstler
Cove Neck
Oyster Bay, New York 11771

Dear Mr. Kunstler:

By now your painting of "Custer Last Stand" should have returned safely to you. I could only find two apparent errors regarding historical accuracy. Standing to the right of Cooke there is one soldier who is wearing a holster on the left side. Military regulations require this to be worn on the right side, butt forward in the holster. The other error is not so obvious. You show two men wearing crossed sabres with what looks like company letters or the numeral seven. I think to avoid an argument I would have omitted the letter or number designations altogether since the preponderance of evidence suggests the enlisted men were not using them in 1876.

Mort, let me tell you with all candor how much I admire your painting! From an historical perspective it is as accurate as any that I have seen.

From the uniforms and equipment to the landscape and the horizon, I think you have captured the very essence of the futility and hopelessness of the battle that symolizes the public's perception of the struggle. It, unquestionably, is the freshest approach and should supersede all others at once.

Sincerely,

Neil C. Mangum
Chief Historian

"TAKE PRIDE IN AMERICA"

Critics Praise

CENTENNIAL CAMPAIGN
The Sioux War of 1876

"I have no hesitation in labelling this the best single volume ever published on the Custer Battle and the Sioux War of 1876."—Robert M. Utley. "In its soundly documented and absorbing book John Gray manages with cumulative power what few have attempted: a total view of the U.S. Army campaign against the Sioux in 1876—that strange wilderness war whose center piece was the Custer 'massacre.' There's no nonsense here, no romantic pseudo-history. Gray uses authentic sources with critical insight, cuts his slices cleanly and bluntly."—*Publishers Weekly*. "A fine book. . . . Gray gives us the whole story in an integrated package. . . . In the twenty-two chapters that comprise the background and the campaign narrative, the author is at his best when he moves away from the Washington scene to detail the field operations. But it is the second part of the book—seven chapters labeled "Puzzles"—that moves Centennial Campaign into the realm of the exceptional. Here Dr. Gray combines impressive research, careful analysis, and sound deduction to reconstruct Indian movements, locations, and concentrations."—*Western Historical Quarterly*. "[Gray's] views are occasionally controversial, but are based on a careful consideration of the primary material. By revealing the many garbled secondary accounts, he brings some fresh insights to the issues. A series of good maps helps the reader follow campaign activity. This is a thoughtful study of a tragic, unnecessary war."—Roger L. Nichols, *Journal of American History*.

John S. Gray, a retired medical doctor and professor of physiology, became interested in American frontier history as a respite from university administrative duties. Robert M. Utley, author of the Foreword and of many books on western American history, retired as Deputy Executive Director of the President's Advisory Council on Historic Preservation. John A. Popovich, creator of the much-praised maps in *Centennial Campaign*, is a retired oil-company executive and several times president of the Custer Battlefield Historical and Museum Association.

"Custer's Last Stand" by Mort Kunstler reflects the final moments of the 7th Cavalry under Custer. Photo courtesy of Hammer Galleries, N. Y.

University of Oklahoma Press
Norman, Oklahoma 73019

ISBN 0-8061-2152-1

GRAY

Oklahoma

CENTENNIAL CAMPAIGN
The Sioux War
of 1876

BY JOHN S. GRAY
Foreword by Robert M. Utley
Maps by John A. Popovich

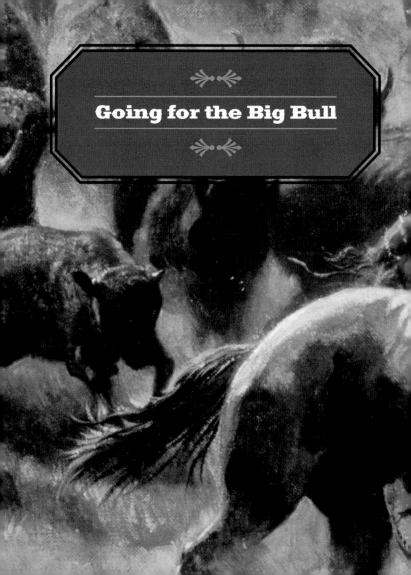

Going for the Big Bull

Stripped down to a breechcloth and moccasins, riding bareback, Indian hunters always made a buffalo herd's leader their first target. The lead buffalo often stood seven feet at the shoulder and weighed about one ton. Buffalo are extremely near-sighted and dim-witted herd animals that, on the death of their leader, will immediately accept leadership from the first male that fights the attacking hunters or makes a run for safety. Indian hunters immediately killed each male that asserted itself, until a herd was dominated by cows. The cows, usually standing about five feet at the shoulder and weighing between seven and nine hundred pounds, were much less dangerous and more easily killed.

The Indians had highly trained buffalo ponies that they controlled by knee pressure. They would often ride bareback and carry only a bow, a quiver of arrows, and a knife. Each hunter had his own distinctive arrow so that it could be determined who had killed each buffalo. A common tactic in this kind of terrain would be to use the rocky outcroppings to funnel the herd through a narrow space, making it easier to kill them. Stampeding the buffalo over a cliff was another often-used practice. For many tribes, the buffalo was the main source of food, clothing, and shelter.

In the 1870s, the Sharps Firearms Company produced the "Big Fifty," a rifle that rested on a bipod and fired .50 caliber slugs. White buffalo hunters set up the big gun on hills overlooking buffalo herds and shot the leader and each assertive male in turn until they annihilated the herd. Between 1872 and 1874, mounted Indians armed with light rifles, bows and arrows, or lances killed an estimated 1.2 million buffalo. During that same period white hunters armed with Big Fifties took out approximately 4.4 million bison.

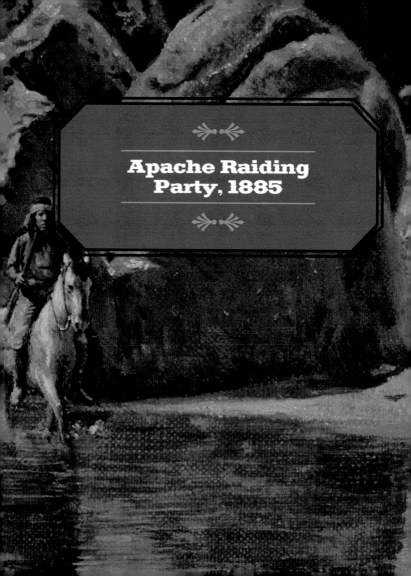

Apache Raiding
Party, 1885

Apache Raiding Party was conceived
in 1977 during a trip to Arizona and New Mexico. I had rented a car
and was traveling all over the Southwest looking for material to incor-
porate into future paintings. I came across a small lake and rocky outcropping that intrigued me. When I heard that Apache had raided in
this part of Arizona during the 1880s, I immediately envisioned this
scene. I made preliminary sketches on the spot, took some photographs, and after returning to my studio, began the painting.

The warrior on the left wears a captured cavalry jacket, more as a
trophy than as clothing. The Apache are well armed with '73 Win-
chesters, pistols, and sabers, and some have cavalry saddles—all signs
of success from recent raids.

Of the six great Apache tribes, the Chiricahua of New Mexico and
Arizona may have fought the U.S. cavalry the longest and hardest.
Cochise, Mangas Colorados, Victorio, Nana, and Geronimo were some
of their most famous and cunning leaders. Of these, Geronimo made
the biggest impression on the American public and news media.

After a lifetime as a raider and warrior, fifty-year-old Geronimo
was arrested in 1877 and held at the San Carlos, Arizona, reservation.
In 1881 he escaped for the first time and, with a band of loyal braves,
conducted raids in New Mexico, southern Arizona, and northern
Mexico. With no more than a couple of dozen raiders riding with him
at any time, Geronimo regularly dodged thousands of U.S. and Mexican troops and threatened isolated ranches and settlements. With no
permanent base the raider grew tired and was persuaded to surrender
by Maj. Gen. George Crook in February 1884; however, his three-year
run from the reservation would not be his last.

Storm Clouds

Key drawing plate on mylar for serigraph

I came across these rocks during one of my trips through South Dakota and Wyoming. As I walked around and looked up, I thought a painting of Sioux warriors, standing on the rocks and silhouetted against the sky, would be dramatic. The idea then came to me of painting storm clouds in the background, symbolic of the storms of conflict that were in the future as this small scouting party watches the white settlers encroach on their lands.

Armed with a traditional Sioux lance, carrying nothing taken from white soldiers, the braves in this painting could be some of the Ogalala Sioux of Red Cloud's tribe in the 1860s. Under the leadership of Red Cloud, the Sioux successfully resisted an invasion of whites who used the Bozeman Trail to reach the Montana gold fields. The trail ran directly through Sioux hunting grounds. During the Civil War, the federal government tried to protect the trail to keep much-needed gold coming from the West and supplies going to the miners, and so the army set up Forts Smith, Kearny, and Reno along the trail. Red Cloud formed alliances with other Sioux and also with the Cheyenne and the Arapaho. The Sioux terrorized the trail through 1865 and pursued a war with the army through 1866. After negotiating with the Sioux in 1867, the government abandoned the Bozeman Trail the following year and many of the Sioux were relocated to reservations farther west. This conflict was the last in which the Sioux were clear winners.

When the transcontinental railroad was completed in 1869 with its route fixed in iron, there would be no more concessions. The unrelenting tide of white settlers overwhelmed the tribes and their ancient ways. The Sioux and their fellow tribes on the plains were forced to make way for the iron horse.

Cheyenne Winter

This was the first of three paintings I did in the early 1980s depicting a raiding party. *Cheyenne Winter* gave me a chance to create a tranquil snow scene, while at the same time use the warriors coming out of the shadows to give the viewer a sense of impending violence. A patch of sunlight coming through the snow-laden trees of the forest allowed me to use the brightest colors in the painting on the two leading braves. The third warrior in line, who is about to come into the sunlight, is a member of the Red Shield society of dog soldiers.

Discipline and tactical planning for war fell to the dog soldiers, members of fraternal warrior societies inside the Cheyenne tribes. One of their traditional assignments was to fight rear-guard actions. During one conflict, each dog soldier drove a stake into the frozen earth and tied his ankle to it with a leather thong, showing his commitment to his duty. In that fight each dog soldier died at his stake.

The men shown here are Cheyenne in winter war paint. Winter was not a battle season, but from the 1860s onward, the time and place of war were the choosing of the whites, not the Cheyenne's.

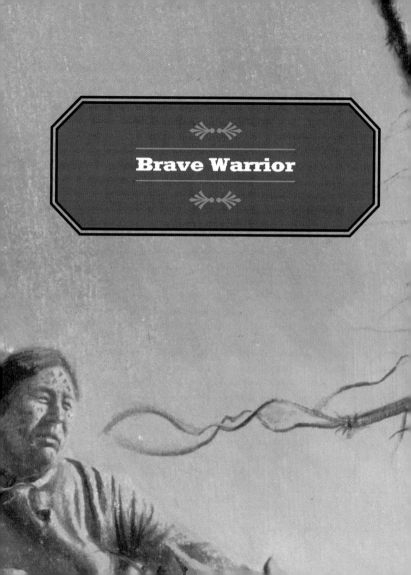

Brave Warrior

The third painting I did in 1979 on Plains Indians charging on horseback was *Brave Warrior*. For an artist, it is challenging to take the same subject matter, especially when intrigued by it, and make several completely different paintings. In *Brave Warrior* I used a very low eye level to give the warrior a heroic look and came in close for a more detailed focus. I completed the painting just in time for my one-man show at Hammer Galleries in New York City on October 22, 1979. The painting was still wet when it was hung for the opening night preview, and it was sold that night.

Everything the warrior wears or carries is made from hide, hair, wood, or bone. He is adorned with the eagle feather, which is a mark of bravery. His small, round shield is of particular interest. Decorated with a picture of a buffalo calf, it would have been made of two or three layers of buffalo hide. It could not spare the warrior from bullets, but it could sometimes deflect stone-tipped arrows like those clutched by the rider beside him in this scene. The quirt tied to the warrior's right wrist was probably also made from buffalo hide. His bridle would have been made of woven horsehair.

The long, curved staff he carries is a coup stick. The ancient practice of touching an enemy with a stick, instead of killing him, demonstrated a warrior's bravery and deadliness. The name attached to the practice is French, because in early contacts with these tribes French observers noted the practice of striking the enemy with the staff and called the hits "coups" or blows. Around the campfire, warriors entertained each other and competed for higher status in the tribe by reciting their deeds of bravery. Recalling the number of times they had slain or struck an enemy was called "counting coup."

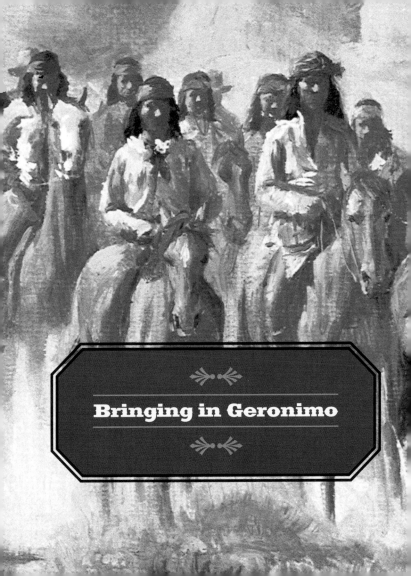

Bringing in Geronimo

In 1978, I explored southern Arizona and New Mexico where Geronimo and his Apache warriors raided. I took many photographs of the scenery and, in 1984, had the idea of painting Geronimo being brought in by cavalry. My aim was to create a beautiful desert landscape showing the terrain through which Geronimo was tracked. This scene is not a specific surrender but could be any one of the times that he was captured.

The Apache chief made a name for himself as a raider in the 1870s. He consistently outmaneuvered his pursuers, despite their superior forces. The media reported Geronimo's reputed depredations in bold headlines and his name became as familiar to newspaper readers in New York City as it was to the panicked ranchers of Arizona, New Mexico, and Chihuahua.

On September 3, 1886 Geronimo and his band surrendered to Maj. Gen. Nelson A. Miles. Military authorities were chagrined to discover his entire war party numbered just fifty men and a few women. They were sent to Alabama and Florida where many caught malaria or tuberculosis and died. Geronimo was regarded as a prisoner of war, not a criminal. After confinement in a Florida prison camp, he moved to Fort Sill, Oklahoma. Later he traveled widely, appearing at fairs and expositions where he sold autographed souvenirs.

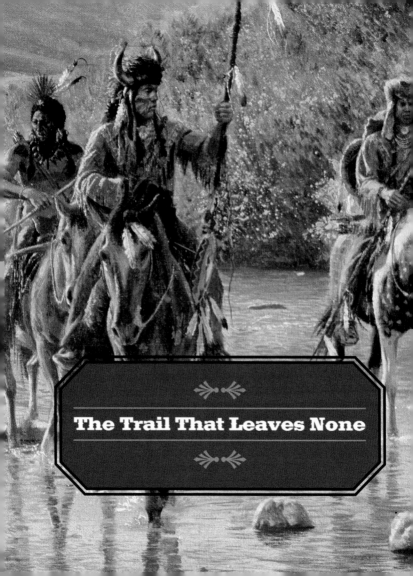

The Trail That Leaves None

In 1875 and 1876 the northern
Cheyenne tribes left the area the U.S. government had given them on
the Sioux Reservation in the South Dakota badlands and roamed
through Wyoming and Montana. While raiding and hunting during
those months, they were pursued by cavalry troopers who followed
scouts recruited from the Crow tribe, traditional rivals of the Cheyenne.

The time in this painting is the mid-1870s. The prized '73 Winchester carried by the leading warrior attests to that. The place is the
North Platte River in Wyoming. A war party of Cheyenne is using a
system of streams as a water trail, allowing easy riding without leav-
ing any signs for Crow or cavalry to follow. I walked and rode up and
down the river near Encampment, Wyoming searching for the right
scenic spot before finding this location.

My idea was to show a tranquil landscape, giving the painting a
peaceful feeling, but at the same time use the Indians at the center of
the painting to imply violence in the near future. They are fitted out
in raiding gear, and they move down the stream with deadly preci-
sion, their trail impossible to detect.

This painting was done as a natural sequel to *Cheyenne Winter.*
Both paintings show the different weather conditions in which the
raiding parties operated.

When You Can't
Hide Your Tracks

I conceived this painting to show

how various weather conditions influenced the outcome of many encounters between Indians and the whites. I wanted to bring out two focal points to tell the story: the cavalry and the hiding Indian. To call attention to the pursuing troopers, I placed them in the visual center, silhouetting them against a clear patch of sky and using a tree's branches to point to them. I also made the sky warm at that spot to contrast with the cool blue grays of the snow.

It was easier to call attention to the concealed Indian. Although in shadows, he and his exhausted horse are large, and I put some bright color on them. The footprints in the snow lead the viewer's eye to them. We know the Indian will not escape, but we do not know if he will surrender or fight to the death, which brings tension into the otherwise tranquil scene.

For centuries, western Indians spent the months when snow lay on the ground inside lodges, eating smoked fish and dried meat, mending tools and weapons, and performing meditative religious rites. However, winter made their struggle with whites more difficult. It was during winter that Chief Joseph and the Nez Percé surrendered with this famous declaration: "Our chiefs are killed. . . . It is cold and we have no blankets. The little children are freezing to death. My people, some of them, have run away to the hills, and have no blankets, no food; no one knows where they are, perhaps freezing to death. I want to have time to look for my children and see how many I can find. . . . My heart is sick and sad. From where the sun now stands, I will fight no more forever."

Buffalo Hunt

This is the second of the two buffalo hunt paintings I did in 1982 that I eventually used as a study for my major oil, *Splitting the Herd*. Charles Russell did approximately sixty Indian buffalo hunt paintings, and so I guess I am not the only artist intrigued by this subject. After finally completing *Splitting the Herd*, I vowed not to do another buffalo painting. Of course, Russell probably said the same thing after he did his first five.

In this scene, a mounted hunter armed with a bow and arrow prepares to release a killing shot on a buffalo. He is aiming for a spot directly behind the animal's last rib. Other killing spots were the bison's diaphragm and lungs. Even after a successful hit, the frightened animal could still travel a mile before he dropped.

Another method of buffalo hunting was practiced by native Americans before the coming of the horse. Buffalo in a herd are ferocious and do not fear wolves traveling singly or in pairs. Indian hunters would don wolf pelts and, moving upwind of a herd, crawl on hands and knees toward their prey. Once in range, they dispatched the targeted buffalo with a short, stout lance or an arrow fired by a three-foot bow.

These tactics were first observed by white hunters late in the eighteenth century, but such daring hunt scenes did not capture the popular imagination for a few more decades. In the 1830s Swiss artist Karl Bodmer and Philadelphia painter George Catlin observed tribal life and preserved what they saw on canvas.

The Chase

This is the first of two buffalo hunt paintings I did in 1982, and explores other composition possibilities after I had finished *Going for the Big Bull*. I utilized some of the elements in this painting on my major canvas, *Splitting the Herd*.

Each spring from 1870 onward, railroaders, farmers, cattlemen, sportsmen, and commercial hunters had tracked down the buffalo. After 1883 no Plains Indian warrior would know the thrill of the buffalo hunt again.

The demands on the herds were too great. Soon, where roaming bands of Indians had found buffalo herds, they found only fields of bleached bones. Then to the amazement of the white hunters, at the start of the 1883 season neither they nor the Indians found any bison. It was as if the species had disappeared entirely.

Historians combing naturalists' records have discovered the demise of the buffalo was not entirely the hunters' fault. Cattle diseases struck the herds, grazing land was destroyed, and droughts killed animals in large numbers as early as the 1840s. The railroads doomed the vast herds by halving the buffalo's migratory range.

The Challenge

Rocky outcroppings have always fascinated me. When I see rocks with interesting shapes or unique lighting effects, they always seem to inspire a painting. On seeing this particular grouping on one of my many trips to the West, I saw the potential for a painting similar to *Storm Clouds*. Instead of the dark, stormy sky in that painting, I used a peaceful blue sky with puffy white clouds to contrast the threatening, ominous gesture of the chief warrior.

Northern plains tribesmen, fitted out and painted for war, extend a challenge to an enemy. Skilled Indian opponents would know these warriors represent a small segment of a larger attacking force concealed somewhere behind or beneath the rocks. In their many wars with the northern plains tribes, the U.S. cavalry did not always understand this practice and paid dearly for their ignorance.

One famous example of the army's misreading the number of Indians prepared to fight was the battle of the Little Bighorn in 1876. On that occasion George Custer believed the smaller force he first confronted was merely a raiding party. It proved to be bait for an army of Sioux and Cheyenne numbering as many as fifteen hundred.

Another example was the Fetterman Massacre of December 1866. On that occasion, a wood-cutting party from Fort Kearny, Wyoming, was attacked by a small party of Sioux, Cheyenne, and Arapaho. The wood cutters were allowed to escape. In retaliation, the fort's commander immediately dispatched a force of eighty men under Lt. Col. William Fetterman to take on the Indians. Unknown to Fetterman or the fort's commander, just out of sight an overwhelming force of warriors waited to attack. Every man of Fetterman's force was killed.

Apache Roundup

The Apache were the most proficient horsemen in the far Southwest. In Apache tribal culture—as in the cultures of most of the western tribes—the horse conferred status and economic power. When he married, an Apache male was expected to bring a certain number of horses to his intended bride's family before his proposal could be considered. In the sixteenth century horses became an indispensable part of the Apache way of life. With their skill on horseback, the Apache plagued their enemies on the plains with deadly, lightning-fast raids.

The Apache could ride their horses into the ground when necessary, and so their need for fresh mounts was constant. The economic appetite for horses shared by the six major Apache tribes seemed insatiable. They stole horses from the Spanish, the Mexicans, the Texans, the Commanche, the Navaho, the U.S. cavalry, and the Mexican military as well as from settlers, trappers, and miners.

In this painting, a group of hard-riding braves rounds up a herd of horses in a box canyon. In spite of all their knowledge and equine expertise, the tribes never bred horses on a large scale. The nomadic, warring ways of most tribes made this skill impractical. If they were pressed, however, the Apache would capture and break the tough, wild horses that roamed the Southwest.

The Apache in the foreground, whipping his mount, is riding a captured cavalry horse, which would not be his first choice for this sort of operation. His use of the less-well-trained horse shows his tribe's desperate need for new horses.

Survivors

This 1981 painting depicts the return of a Sioux warrior after a raid. He has lost a companion but managed to bring back the warrior's horse. A warrior returning from a raid with his companion's horse but not his body meant extraordinary grief for the warrior's family. Using the river to lose his pursuers, he makes his way back to his village and will fight another day.

The war paint on both the man and the horses was significant. The circles around the horses' eyes were meant to give them better sight during battle. Hoof marks were meant to give the animal additional speed. Each warrior had his own individual markings.

The coup stick the warrior carries was not used to kill an enemy but rather to humiliate him by getting close enough to touch him. The warrior would strike him with the stick, showing that he could kill him at any time. The number of feathers in a warbonnet often were a record of the number of coup that a warrior had counted. A popular misconception is that only chiefs wore bonnets.

Among the Plains Indians, death in battle brought honor. It was best if the slain warrior could be put to rest by his own people. The body, along with the warrior's finest arms and possessions, was wrapped in a shroud and placed in a tree or on a scaffold and left to deteriorate naturally. If the death occurred on the open prairie, the wrapped body was heaped over with stones. In either case, the warrior's family wept copiously and mourned loudly. In some tribes the deceased's best war or hunting pony was put to death so that it could accompany him in the afterlife.

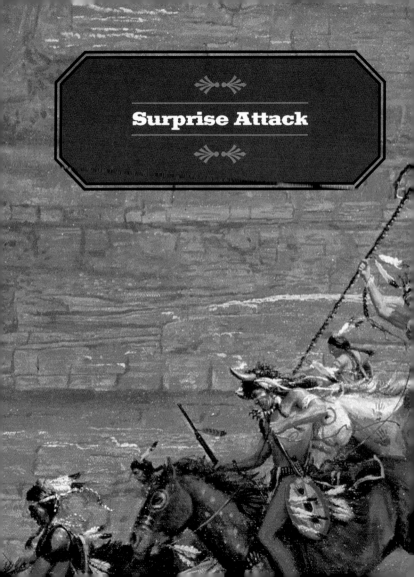

Surprise Attack

After creating western paintings for a number of years, I concluded that one of the most exciting, action-packed subjects I could paint would be Plains Indians in an all-out charge. My first painting on this theme was *War Cry.* I enjoyed it so much that I immediately embarked on a similar painting. The challenge was to make it interesting and exciting, like *War Cry,* but to achieve a totally different look. The Indians in *War Cry* were coming right at the viewer, and so my first thought was to have the Indians in the next painting shown in profile. Instead of a flat, dry riverbed as the terrain, I realized it would be better to have the braves charging down the side of a mountain. Instead of using bright, unfiltered sunlight, I created a sharp contrast of light and shade caused by a low sun and the surrounding mountains.

All the great war chiefs of the West knew the advantages of surprise and mobility. This scene, showing Plains Indians bearing down on their enemies from the rocky heights, was repeated in battle after battle and was usually successful.

In the great summer campaign against the Sioux and Cheyenne in Montana in 1876, Gen. George Crook's force of thirteen hundred troops and Crow and Shoshoni allies was attacked in the base of a small valley near the head of Rosebud Creek by a larger number of Sioux and Cheyenne charging down from the ridges above. Most of the white soldiers and their allies survived the battle, but not without some luck and the expenditure of twenty-five thousand rounds of ammunition. Although they did not send the army into retreat, the Sioux and Cheyenne considered the encounter a victory. They had stopped the white forces in their tracks.

Return of the Raiders

After painting *Survivors,* my thoughts turned to what it must have been like during a retreat from an unsuccessful raid. What would happened several hours before the scene in *Survivors*? While the raider in *Survivors* has reached relative safety, this painting captures the danger of the chase and the chance of capture and death after a confrontation.

I have always enjoyed using the interesting shapes of rocks as a design element. The patterns of light and dark that they create adds to the composition to give the feeling that the raiding party can lose itself in this rocky maze and escape any pursuers.

If the enemy were from a hostile tribe, the result of capture was probably torture and death. If the pursuers were white, the results could be the same or imprisonment. Indian raiders captured by U.S. cavalry troops were sometimes placed in confinement on a reservation; other times they were imprisoned in facilities in Florida, Alabama, or Oklahoma.

The Vanishing American

This painting, done in 1981, was among the last I created specifically to illustrate a book cover. It was commissioned for the Zane Grey novel *The Vanishing American*, which was published the following year. Despite the many restrictions imposed on a painting for a book cover, this still remains one of my favorites.

The problems in painting an illustration for a book cover are numerous. First, the artist must tell the story. This particular story was about a young Indian who was educated in a white school and became an acclaimed athlete and scholar before he returned to his homeland. This book was about the end of an era.

To capture both ideas, I dressed the main character in traditional Indian clothing but gave him a white man's hat. I put him on a white man's horse instead of a scrawny Indian pony. I chose twilight to convey the idea that the era of tribal life on the plains was in its twilight years.

Second, the center of interest must be on the right of the painting, because that side would be the front cover of the book; the left side would be the back cover. By painting night light on the left, the blue tones allowed all of the copy on the back of the book to be printed in white, which is easily read. There also has to be adequate space on the top right side to print the book title and author's name. These problems lead to restrictions on the artist that very often end up with less-than-perfect solutions. In this case, however, I believe this painting worked very well as a book cover and equally well on its own as a painting.

Portrait Gallery

❖

In this collection of seven portraits of tribal leaders I attempt to show the diversity of the Indian peoples in North America. The most popular image of the native American is that of the Sioux warrior wearing a long, feathered warbonnet. *Chief High Horse* resulted from a trip I took to the Rosebud Sioux Reservation in South Dakota, and it is a depiction of a Sioux in his traditional dress.

The portraits *Beaded Headband* and *The Future, The Past* are also from my trip to the Rosebud Sioux. There was a significant difference in the clothing, facial characteristics, customs, and language of the Sioux and the California Maidu as represented in the painting of *Osabaki and Butu.*

While I was on a trip to Sacramento, Marie Potts, Osabaki's grandmother, consented to pose for me even though she was ill. A truly remarkable woman, she was the first native American woman to receive a college degree. She died in 1977.

The diversity of the Indian nations is even more apparent when one compares *Apache Scout,* an Apache from the Southwest, and *Haida Headman,* a warrior from the Northwest coast.

All the tribes developed and adapted to their environment remarkably well over thousands of years. Each had its own language, religion, customs, art, and political alliances. Whether technologically advanced, highly civilized, or primitive, all suffered the same fate of being overwhelmed by the whites within only a few hundred years.

Haida Headman

MARIE POTTS, CHENKUTPEM OF THE MAIDU

CHIEF HIGH HORSE

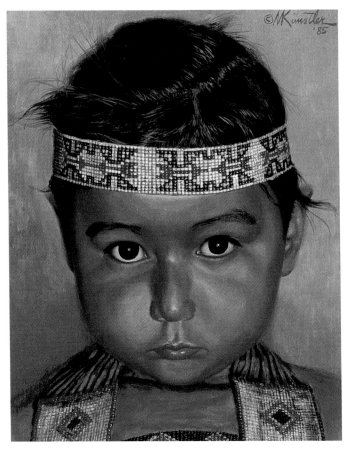

BEADED HANDBAND

OSOBAKI AND BUTU

APACHE SCOUT

THE FUTURE, THE PAST

Acknowledgments

With special thanks to:

Larry Stone, Ed Curtis, and Peaches Scribner of Rutledge Hill Press
for suggesting the idea of publishing twin volumes on cowboys and
Indians. As usual, it has been a pleasure to work with them, and I am
grateful for their encouragement and understanding.

Richard Lynch of Hammer Galleries in New York City, for giving me
my first one-man show in 1977 and for bringing my paintings to the
attention of the art world.

Howard Shaw and the rest of the staff at Hammer Galleries.

Jane Künstler Broffman and Paula McEvoy, for their invaluable help,
not only with this book but in the everyday tasks of managing a busy
studio.

My dear Deborah, the wind beneath my wings.